Brush With Greatness

Monet

Tamra B. Orr

PURPLE TOAD
PUBLISHING

Copyright © 2017 by Purple Toad Publishing, Inc. All rights reserved. No part of this book may be reproduced without written permission from the publisher. Printed and bound in the United States of America.

Printing   1   2   3   4   5   6   7   8   9

Goya
Leonardo da Vinci
Michelangelo
Monet
Van Gogh

Publisher's Cataloging-in-Publication Data
Orr, Tamra.
   Monet / written by Tamra Orr.
      p. cm.
Includes bibliographic references, glossary, and index.
ISBN 9781624691973
1. Monet, Claude, 1840-1926—Juvenile literature. 2. Painters—France—Biography—Juvenile literature. I. Series: Brush with greatness.
   ND553.M7 2017
   759.4

eBook ISBN: 9781624691980

Library of Congress Control Number: 2016937172

ABOUT THE AUTHOR: Tamra Orr is a full-time writer and author living in the Pacific Northwest. She has written more than 400 nonfiction educational books for all ages. She loves learning about the world, from exotic locations and animals to fascinating people in history. When she is not writing books, she is reading books and writing letters—or looking through art books and marveling at how artists can help you see the world in all new ways.

Contents

Chapter 1
Monsieur Monet 5

Chapter 2
Like a Prison 9

Chapter 3
"A Veil Torn Away" 13

Chapter 4
The Mighty Trains 19

Chapter 5
Inspiring Others 23

Timeline 28
Selected Works 29
Further Reading 30
Glossary 31
Index 32

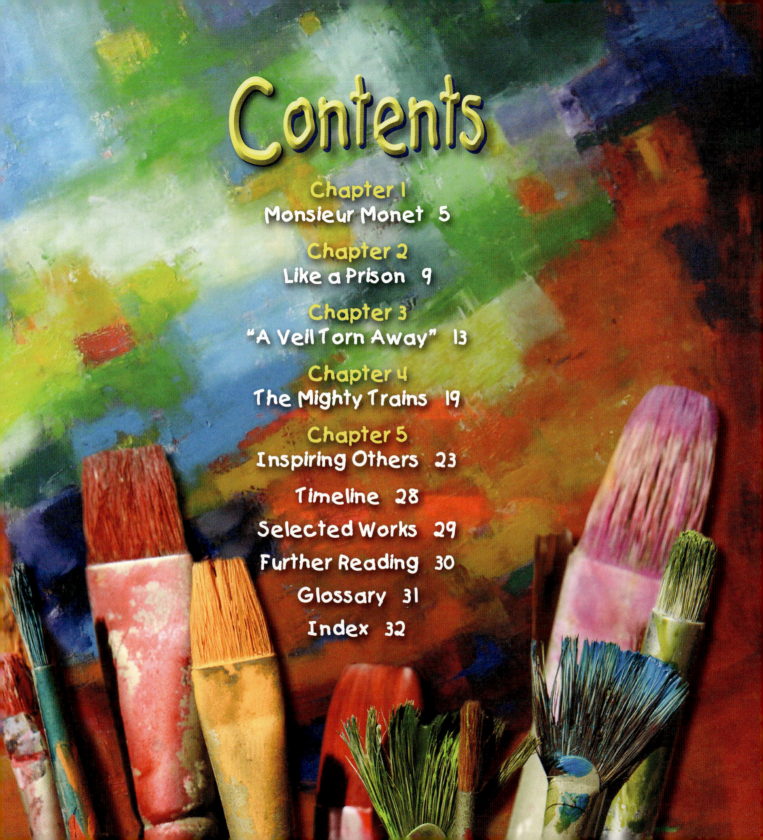

Chapter 1
Monsieur Monet

"Gabriel!" my mother called. Hurry up! You are going to be late."

I scrambled out of bed, and threw on my clothes and shoes. "Go quickly, and be sure to report to Monsieur **(miz-YUR)** Lafette."

Today was my first day to work at the busiest train station in Paris. I was to sweep the platforms where people got on and off the trains. The soot from the trains made the ground dirty. Passengers do not like stepping off onto a sooty platform — especially the women! They yank up their dresses so high, my father said, you can see their ankles.

Walking into the station, I felt goosebumps all over. People were coming and going. Trains were rumbling. I wanted to stay here forever.

"Ah, Mr. Gabriel—*there* you are," said Monsieur Lafette sternly. "Here is your broom. Follow me. I have a special place for you to begin sweeping." We went outside and I saw a man standing on the platform. He was clearly not a passenger! He had an easel with a large canvas on it for painting. He had a thick, bushy beard and wore a black hat called a beret.

He glanced over and frowned. "Monsieur Monet **(moh-NAY)**, this is Gabriel," said Lafette. "He is here to keep your area clean." The bearded man growled a reply. "Gabriel, this is the famous artist Claude Monet. Treat him with the utmost respect."

I nodded, but all I could think about was that growl.

Monet's paintings of the trains coming and going captured the noise and power in the station.

Chapter 2
Like a Prison

Keeping my head down, I swept until the floor around Monsieur Monet was spotless. Just as I finished, the artist packed up his equipment. He strapped the easel to his back and tucked his canvas under his arm, careful not to touch any wet paint. "Follow me," he said.

Follow him? Why?

"I have a room near here," Monet explained. "It is nothing much—a small room on the ground floor. You shall carry my paint box for me. We shall talk on the way."

I nodded, afraid to speak. A small smile lit Monet's face. "Do not worry—I growl but do not bite. Do you like school?" he asked. I shook my head. "When I was a child, I would run away from school every chance I got," the artist admitted. "I would go to the nearby ocean," he added. "I love the sea. I would sit by the water and draw cartoons of my teachers." He smiled, remembering. "Finally, at age 11, I went to art school—and my life changed. Shall I tell you how?"

All I could do was nod.

A Monet cartoon and his painting, *The Cliff Walk*, 1882

The Beach at Villerville, 1864, by the artist Eugene Boudin inspired Monet to see the world in a different way.

Chapter 3
"A Veil Torn Away"

"I loved art school," continued Monet, "but it was not school that changed me. It was meeting another artist. His name was Eugène Boudin (**ew-JEN boo-DEHN**). One day, I was watching him paint and something wonderful happened." He closed his eyes for a moment. "Suddenly a veil was torn away," he said, opening his eyes wide. "I had understood—I had realized what painting could be. By the single example of this painter devoted to his art with such independence, my destiny as a painter opened out to me."

Jean Monet on his Hobby Horse (Claude Monet's son) and *Woman With A Parasol* (Monet's wife), *Water Lilies and Japanese Bridge*.

He unlocked his front door. "You see, Boudin showed me the beauty that was around me—in the fields of poppies, the ponds with floating water lilies, the rows of poplar trees. I painted my wife and sons at rest and play."

"I began painting outside. I studied how the light changed everything, and how everyday moments were perfect for painting." He pulled me back outside to the alley behind his room.

Monet's *The Summer Poppy Field* shows how strongly he paid attention to light and shadows when he painted.

"Look at the light on the wall there," he said. He turned me around. "Look at the sunshine on the trees. Now, the sun is starting to set. Watch what happens."

As we stood together watching the sun slowly sink in the sky, it was like looking through someone else's eyes.

"See how the yellow turns to gold?" whispered Monet. "Watch as shades of orange light up the leaves."

He was right. It was as if the light were a giant paintbrush, changing everything around me.

I would never see my city the same way again.

Madame Monet and Child explodes with color and different shades of blue.

Chapter 4
The Mighty Trains

It was getting late and I knew my mother would be worried, but I had to ask Monet one question before going home.

"But sir, if you paint the world around you, why do you live here, surrounded by the soot and smoke of the trains?"

Monet paused. "As much as I loved my paintings, the critics did not. They said the colors were too bright—the scenes . . . not real enough." He sighed. "Those were dark days. I destroyed many paintings, even tossing them into the fire. But now," he added, the sadness fading from his face, "I have found a new idea—the trains."

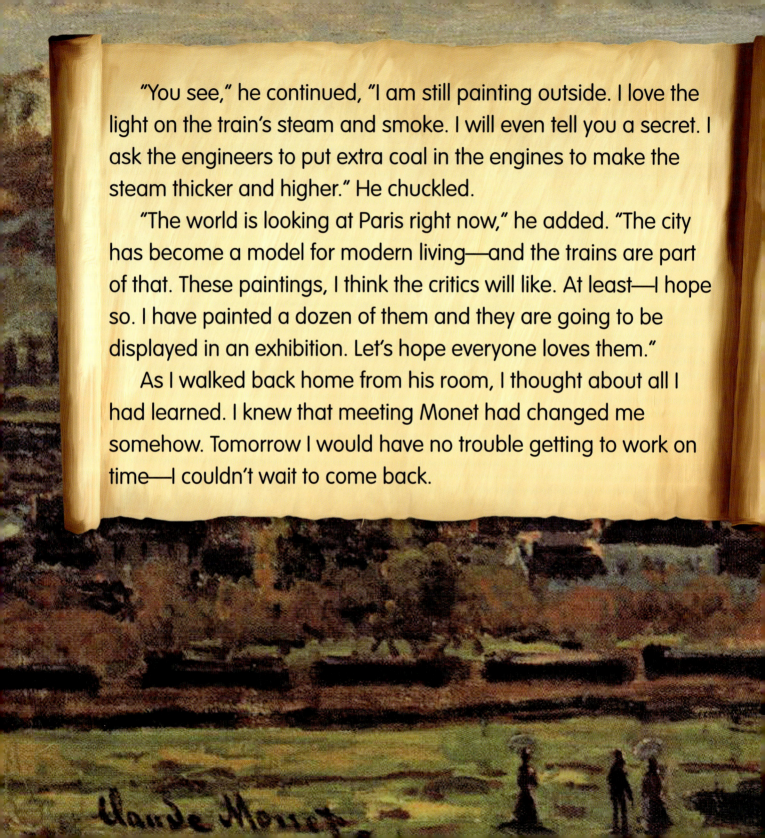

"You see," he continued, "I am still painting outside. I love the light on the train's steam and smoke. I will even tell you a secret. I ask the engineers to put extra coal in the engines to make the steam thicker and higher." He chuckled.

"The world is looking at Paris right now," he added. "The city has become a model for modern living—and the trains are part of that. These paintings, I think the critics will like. At least—I hope so. I have painted a dozen of them and they are going to be displayed in an exhibition. Let's hope everyone loves them."

As I walked back home from his room, I thought about all I had learned. I knew that meeting Monet had changed me somehow. Tomorrow I would have no trouble getting to work on time—I couldn't wait to come back.

Some of Monet's train paintings showed the train from a distance, the smoke filling the air.

Chapter 5
Inspiring Others

Gabriel worked with Monet during a turning point in the artist's life. By the time Monet finished painting trains, he had also completed *Impression: Sunrise* (1872). A newspaper editor called his style "impressionist" and the name stuck. Monet, and the artists who copied him, were called Impressionists (im-PRESH-uh-nists).

> It was with the bright colors and shadows of Monet's *Impression: Sunrise* that earned some artists a new name.

Impressionists used short brush strokes of bright colors to show the effect of light on objects. Monet's haystack paintings (1890–1891) were a perfect example of this style. Although each painting showed haystacks in fields, each one was unique because of the play of light and colors on them.

Depending on the time of day, the haystacks and Monet's paintings of them looked different.

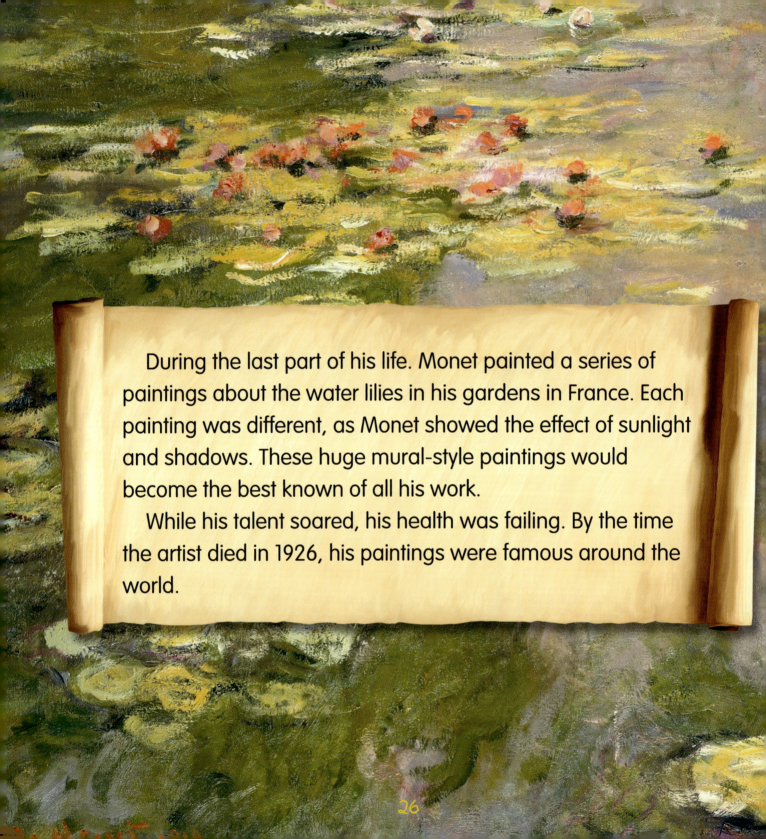

During the last part of his life. Monet painted a series of paintings about the water lilies in his gardens in France. Each painting was different, as Monet showed the effect of sunlight and shadows. These huge mural-style paintings would become the best known of all his work.

While his talent soared, his health was failing. By the time the artist died in 1926, his paintings were famous around the world.

Monet's water lily paintings were so large, they could fill an entire wall.

Timeline

1840 — Oscar-Claude Monet (moh-NAY) is born on November 14 in Paris, France.

1850–56 — Monet attends school; meets Boudin.

1859 — Monet moves to Paris to study art.

1861–1862 — Monet serves in the military in Algeria.

1874 — Monet's *Impression: Sunrise* inspires the style known as Impressionism.

1877 — Monet paints trains in the Paris station Gare Saint-Lazare.

1889 — Monet begins his water lily series, which he continues for decades.

1890-91 — Monet focuses on haystack paintings.

1926 — Monet dies on December 5 in Giverny, France.

Selected Works

1866	*Women in the Garden*
1867	*Quai du Louvre* **(Kay-doo-LOOV)**
1872	*Springtime*
1875	*Camille Monet and a Child in the Artist's Garden in Argenteuil*
1875	*Red Boats at Argenteuil*
1882	*Beach in Pourville*
1891	*Stacks of Wheat*
1900	*Water Lily Pond*
1908	*Le Grand Canal*

Monet's *Women in the Garden*

Further Reading

Books

Bjork, Christina. *Linnea in Monet's Garden.* New York, NY: Sourcebooks Jabberwocky, 2012.

Danneberg, Julie. *Monet Paints a Day.* Watertown, Massachusetts: Charlesbridge, 2012.

Krieg, Katherine. *Claude Monet.* Mankato, MN: Child's World, 2014.

Maltbie, P.I. *Claude Monet: The Painter Who Stopped the Trains.* New York, NY: Abrams Books for Young Readers, 2010.

Venezia, Mike. *Claude Monet* (Getting to Know the World's Greatest Artists). New York: Children's Press, 2014.

Waldron, Ann. *Who Was Claude Monet?* New York, NY: Grosset and Dunlap, 2009.

Works Consulted

Brodskaia, Nathalia. *Claude Monet.* New York, NY: Parkstone Press, 2014.

Gariff, David. *The World's Most Influential Painters and the Artists They Inspired.* New York: Barron's Educational Series, New York, NY, 2008.

Metropolitan Museum: *Claude Monet* http://www.metmuseum.org/toah/hd/cmon/hd_cmon.htm

Murray, Elizabeth. *Monet's Passion: Ideas, Inspiration, and Insights from the Painter's Gardens.* Portland: Pomegranate, 2010.

"Oscar-Claude Monet Biography." *Monetalia.* http://www.monetalia.com/biography.aspx

Seitz, William C. *Claude Monet.* New York, NY: Harry Abrams, Inc. Publishers, 2003.

Wildenstein, Daniel. *Monet, or the Triumph of Impressionism.* New York, NY, China: Taschen Publishing, 2014.

Internet Sites

Biography: Claude Monet, Painter http://www.biography.com/people/claude-monet-9411771

Claude Monet Gallery: The Complete Works http://www.claudemonetgallery.org

Glossary

beret (buh-RAY)—A soft cap with a close-fitting headband and wide, round top.

canvas (KAN-vus)—Blank fabric on which many artists paint.

easel (EE-zul)—A stand or frame that holds an artist's canvas.

exhibition (ek-sih-BIH-shun)—A showing or presentation.

Impressionist (im-PREH-shuh-nist)—An artist who paints in spots of color to capture a feeling more than an exact scene.

monsieur (mih-ZYUR)—"Mister" in French.

mural (MYUR-ul)—Usually, a large painting made on or covering a wall.

palette (PAL-et)—A thin oval board used for holding and mixing paints.

parasol (PAYR-uh-sol)—An umbrella used for shade.

quai (KAY)—The French spelling of quay (KEY), a landing or pier for boats.

soot (SUT)—Fine black ash that sifts out of smoke.

PHOTO CREDITS: All pictures—Public Domain. Every measure has been taken to find all copyright holders of material used in this book. In the event any mistakes or omissions have happened within, attempts to correct them will be made in future editions of the book.

Index

Beach at Villerville 12

Boudin, Eugene 12, 13, 15

Cliff Walk, the 11

Haystacks, The 24, 25

Impressionism 23, 24

Impression: Sunrise 23–24

Jean Monet on his Hobby Horse 14

Madame Monet and Child 18

Monet, Claude

   death 26

   critics 19

   school 10, 13

   train series 19–20

Renoir, Pierre-Auguste 8

Summer Poppy Field, The 16

Train, The 21

Water Lilies and Japanese Bridge 15

water lily 26, 27

Woman with a Parasol 15